House of Portraits

Powis Castle

John Chu

Detail of Joshua Reynolds (1723–92)
Lady Henrietta Herbert (1758–1830)
1777
Oil on canvas
140.3 x 112.3 cm

House of Portraits

Portraits have the power to bring the living face-to-face with the dead.

For centuries the Herberts, one of the most influential families in Welsh history, have had their likenesses captured by artists of outstanding skill. These works of art have been handed down many generations to adorn their ancestral home: Powis Castle. In this house of portraits, people who long ago flourished and passed away appear before us once more, and often look us right in the eye.

Look at them carefully, and these pictures can also tell us about the hopes, passions and ideas of individuals they depict, broadcasting their achievements and sending messages about who they were and how they lived. Long before any celebrity ever posted a selfie, the Herberts were manipulating and projecting their personal image to make a place for themselves in a competitive and sometimes dangerous world of politics, money and power.

Family portraits

The great halls and quiet chambers of Powis Castle are full of pictures of real people. Ranging from majestic full-length portraits to intimate miniatures that can be held in the palm of your hand, they are the work of many talented artists. Some of these faces belong to kings, emperors and maharajas while the identity of others has long ago been lost and forgotten. But the overwhelming majority of these pictures depict men, women and children of the Herbert family who have lived at Powis for over four centuries.

The handing-down of portraits was one of the most important ways in which wealthy and influential families like the Herberts expressed pride in their heritage. To display the images of notable ancestors

was to inspire emulation in the living and to declare to the world that greatness ran in their blood. Rooms in such houses were often built or adapted to accommodate large numbers of portraits so that several generations of the family could be seen in a single glance.

Valued as heirlooms as well as beautiful works of art, portraits tended to be kept together when estates were divided and were among the last assets to be sold when family finances periodically dipped. All kinds of fine pictures once hung in the Herberts' different houses but it is the portrait collection, gathered together at Powis, that has survived to the present in its full glory.

Above: Images of the Herberts have been shown alongside antique busts of Roman emperors in the Long Gallery since at least the 18th century.

Opposite: The family portraits of many generations cover the walls and surfaces of the Blue Drawing Room, including a full-length portrait of Mary Herbert, Marchioness of Powis above the fireplace.

Portraits for a purpose

An ancient portrait collection has the extraordinary ability to describe the appearance of the long-dead but it can also reveal what those people cared about most. The individuals whose images these pictures record were active contributors towards these time-consuming and expensive works of art. They carefully guided their creation to send out powerful and seductive messages about who they were and how they wanted to be seen by the world.

Many of the family portraits at Powis were made for personal and emotional reasons that most people would recognise today: to celebrate a rite of passage such as a marriage or to capture the childhood looks of a son or daughter before they grew up. A portrait might be copied in miniature form and carried around or worn as an expression of love or affection.

Christian Friedrich Zincke
(1685–1767)
*Henry Arthur Herbert,
1st Earl of Powis (1703–67)*
1745–9
Enamel
4.5 x 3.8 cm

This portrait of Henry, 1st Earl of Powis is painted in enamel (coloured glass) and measures only a few centimetres across. It was set among gold and pearls and could be worn as a piece of jewellery.

Suitable to the public stage upon which the Herbert family lived their lives, other portraits project a much grander and more obviously flattering personal image; as valiant warriors, as peoples of taste and fashion, as allies of kings, or as travellers to distant lands. The portraits at Powis Castle reflect the belief of landowning families like the Herberts that leadership was their duty but also their birth-right; they sometimes even appear as the literal embodiments of princely virtues.

Whether intended for public or private use, all kinds of clues are embedded in the costumes, backgrounds, expressions, poses, gestures and frames of these portraits that allow us not only to encounter the dead, but also to understand their point of view. In their eagerness to create exquisitely crafted images of themselves, the Herberts reveal their pressing concern with matters of social status, achievement, posterity and love.

In about 1705 the 2nd Marquess of Powis had his eldest daughters painted on the ceiling of the Library by the Flemish painter Gerard Lanscroon as part of an allegory of good government. Lady Mary appears as Minerva, Goddess of Wisdom, with Lady Theresa holding a mirror at her side representing Truth.

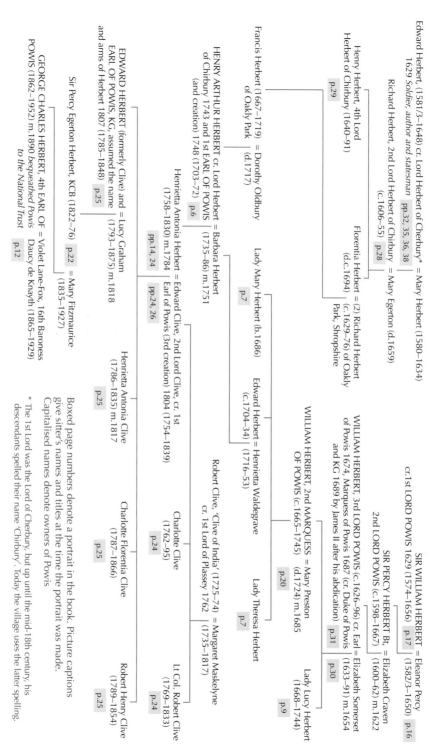

Edward Herbert, (1581/3–1648) cr. Lord Herbert of Cherbury* = Mary Herbert (1580–1634)
1629 Soldier, author and statesman   pp.32, 35, 36, 38

SIR WILLIAM HERBERT 1629 (1574–1656) = Eleanor Percy
cr.1st LORD POWIS   p.17   (1582/3–1650) p.16

Richard Herbert, 2nd Lord Herbert of Chirbury = Mary Egerton (d.1659)
(c.1606–55)   p.28

SIR PERCY HERBERT Bt., = Elizabeth Craven
2nd LORD POWIS (c.1598–1667)   (1600–62) m.1622
p.17

Henry Herbert, 4th Lord Herbert of Chirbury (1640–91)   p.29

Florentia Herbert = (2) Richard Herbert
(d.c.1694)   (c.1629–76) of Oakly Park, Shropshire

WILLIAM HERBERT, 3rd LORD POWIS (c.1626–96) cr. Earl = Elizabeth Somerset
of Powis 1674, Marquess of Powis 1687 (cr. Duke of Powis   (1633–91) m.1654
and KG 1689 by James II after his abdication)   p.31   p.30

Francis Herbert (1667–1719) = Dorothy Oldbury
of Oakly Park   (d.1717)   p.25

HENRY ARTHUR HERBERT cr. Lord Herbert = Barbara Herbert
of Chirbury 1743 and 1st EARL OF POWIS   (1735–86) m.1751
(and creation) 1748 (1703–72)   p.6

Lady Mary Herbert (b.1686)   p.7

WILLIAM HERBERT, 2nd MARQUESS = Mary Preston
OF POWIS (c.1665–1745)   (d.1724) m.1685   p.20

Lady Lucy Herbert (1668–1744)   p.9

Henrietta Antonia Herbert = Edward Clive, 2nd Lord Clive, cr. 1st
(1758–1830) m.1784   Earl of Powis (3rd creation) 1804 (1754–1839)
pp.14, 24   pp.24, 26

Edward Herbert = Henrietta Waldegrave
(1704–34)   (1716–53)

Robert Clive, 'Clive of India' (1725–74) = Margaret Maskelyne
cr. 1st Lord of Plassey 1762   (1735–1817)   p.20

Lady Theresa Herbert   p.7

EDWARD HERBERT (formerly Clive) and = Lucy Graham
EARL OF POWIS, KG., assumed the name   (1793–1875) m.1818
and arms of Herbert 1807 (1785–1848)   p.25

Sir Percy Egerton Herbert, KCB (1822–76)   p.22 = Mary Fitzmaurice
(1835–1927)

Henrietta Antonia Clive
(1786–1835) m.1817
p.25

Charlotte Clive
(1762–95)
p.24

Lt Col. Robert Clive
(1769–1833)
p.24

GEORGE CHARLES HERBERT, 4th EARL OF = Violet Lane-Fox, 16th Baroness
POWIS (1862–1952) m.1890 bequeathed Powis   Daucy de Knayth (1865–1929)
to the National Trust   p.12

Charlotte Florentia Clive
(1787–1866)
p.25

Robert Henry Clive
(1789–1854)
p.25

Boxed page numbers denote a portrait in the book. Picture captions give sitter's names and titles at the time the portrait was made. Capitalised names denote owners of Powis

* The 1st Lord was the Lord of Cherbury, but up until the mid-18th century, his descendants spelled their name 'Chirbury'. Today the village uses the latter spelling.

The Lords of Powis

The first Herberts to live in the castle were the offspring of Sir Edward Herbert, who leased the property in 1578 and bought it soon after. Initially a junior branch of the family of the Earls of Pembroke, the Herberts of Powis rapidly emerged as a force to be reckoned with, amassing honours and great wealth through landholdings in Montgomeryshire and Shropshire. Their fortunes rose and fell most dramatically in the later 17th century when their Catholic faith and closeness to King James II gained them important positions of power but also drove them into exile in France.

When the French artist François de Troy painted this picture of Lady Lucy Herbert, she and her family had gone into exile for their allegiance to the deposed Catholic King James II. She appears in the white robes and veil of a Vestal Virgin: high-born priestesses of ancient Rome who served as public manifestations of female virtue.

François de Troy
(1645–1730)
*Lady Lucy Herbert
(1668–1744)*
1692–3
Oil on canvas
122.5 x 93.5 cm

The Herberts of Chirbury

In the 18th century, the Herberts of Powis were joined through marriage to their distant cousins, the Herberts of Chirbury, who were famous soldiers and men of letters. They brought with them some fine early 17th-century portraits, including an exceptional miniature by Isaac Oliver of the philosopher, poet, diplomat and soldier Edward, 1st Lord Herbert of Cherbury (see page 38).

The Clives

Later in the 18th century a further line of descent was created through marriage to the Clive family, who afterwards adopted the Herbert name and titles. They revived the estate's finances with riches gained through imperial exploits in India. For this reason several likenesses of the controversial soldier and businessman Robert, Lord Clive of Plassey, better known as Clive of India, came to Powis. These arrived with a collection of pictures of Indian princes who sent portraiture as gifts to gain the favour of the Clives.

Indian (Tanjore) School
Maharaja Pratap Singh of Tanjore (c.1739–65)
Late 18th century
Gouache, gold and beetle wing on paper
43 x 35.5 cm

Maharaja Sarabhoji gave this miniature portrait of his grandfather to Lady Henrietta Clive in 1800 when her husband, Lord Edward Clive, was Governor of Madras.

Benjamin West
(1738–1820)
Shah 'Alam, Mughal Emperor, conveying the Grant of the Diwani to Lord Clive, August 1765
c.1818
Oil on canvas
290 x 400 cm
On loan from the British Library

Edward Clive, 1st Earl of Powis, commissioned this very large picture as a tribute to his father's most famous deed. At its centre is a portrait of Clive of India in a red uniform receiving administrative powers (the Diwani) over Bengal, Behar and Orissa from the Mughal Emperor Shah 'Alam. It effectively marked the foundation of British Raj on the subcontinent.

To capture

The basic function of a portrait is to record an individual's outward appearance. In the hands of an exceptional artist portraiture can also capture a sense of that person's presence and inner character.

Here Sargent, darling of Edwardian high society, depicts Violet, wife of George Herbert, 4th Earl of Powis who later bequeathed Powis Castle to the National Trust. The couple renovated the house and gardens from a state of neglect and gave it its present form.

This drawing was made in 1912 when Violet was in the midst of this great project and uses the drama and spontaneity of black charcoal to evoke her dynamism. With one eyebrow raised she casts a piercing gaze over her shoulder, her mouth slightly open as if listening but about to speak.

John Singer Sargent (1856–1925)
Lady Violet Herbert, Countess of Powis and 16th Baroness Darcy de Knayth (1865–1929)
1912
Charcoal on paper
60 x 47.5 cm

Joshua Reynolds
(1723–92)
*Lady Henrietta Herbert
(1758–1830)*
1777
Oil on canvas
140.3 x 112.3 cm

To attract

For high-born young women on the 18th-century marriage market the latest fashions were a must.

Lady Henrietta Herbert, daughter of the Earl of Powis, sat for this portrait by the top London portraitist, Joshua Reynolds, when she was about 19 years old and of an age to marry. The result is one of the most alluring he ever painted.

Seen preparing for a country walk, she puts the finishing touches to her immaculate outfit by pulling on a silk glove. As she sets off, she turns to meet our gaze as if to invite us along.

If you look closely at her hair, the brushstrokes become confused and difficult to read. This is because an earlier smooth hairstyle was painted over with the kind of wide-brimmed hat and wavy hairstyle that became fashionable in the 1780s.

To celebrate

Centuries before the modern wedding photograph there was the pendant marriage portrait.

This pair of pictures is an example of this convention and celebrates the union in 1595 of Lady Eleanor Percy, daughter of the Earl of Northumberland, to William Herbert who was heir to the Powis estate.

Alliances between such high-ranking families were a matter of state importance so it is significant that her costume bears variations on the Tudor rose to signal the couple's allegiance to the ruling dynasty. The precious jewel at Eleanor's breast depicts Cupid and Venus, ancient gods of love and desire, appropriate to the expectation that marriage should produce heirs.

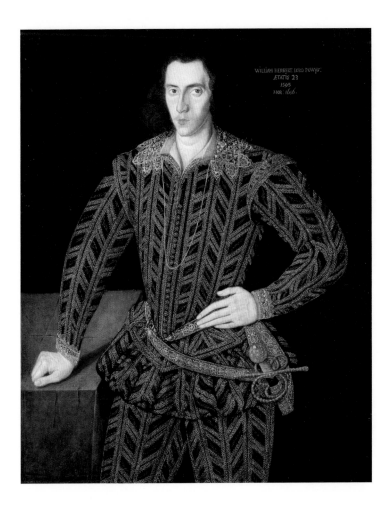

Above: British School
Sir William Herbert (1574–1656)
1595
Oil on canvas
106 x 84 cm

Opposite: British School
Lady Eleanor Herbert (1582/3–1650)
1595
Oil on canvas
106 x 83.8 cm

Attributed to Sebastiano
Bombelli (1635–1719)
*Roger Palmer, 1st Earl of
Castlemaine (1634–1705)*
1664
Oil on canvas
194.3 x 1146 cm

To call home

Portraits can send messages across long distances as well as through time.

The standing figure in this portrait is the 1st Earl of Castlemaine whose maternal grandfather was William Herbert, 1st Lord Powis. The picture was painted in Venice in 1664 when he had sailed to the Middle East with the Venetian fleet – an adventure recorded in the background. The armour piled up in the corner alludes to his military career but his pose is that of an ancient Roman orator as a token of his eloquence.

The letter he is dictating to his secretary is addressed to the Honourable William Herbert (later 1st Marquess of Powis) who was presumably also the recipient of this portrait. It may have been intended as evidence of Castlemaine's honour at a time when his wife was living openly at court as King Charles II's favourite mistress.

Attributed to Charles
d'Agar (1669–1723)
*Mary Herbert, Marchioness
of Powis (d.1724)*
c.1695
Oil on canvas
236.2 x 147.3 cm

To aggrandise

Large portraits such as this presented the public face of the aristocracy and were deliberately designed to keep the viewer at a respectful distance.

Here Mary, wife of the 2nd Marquess of Powis, is shown standing serenely on a terrace of a garden where roses and orange trees grow. This setting alludes to the splendour of the Herbert estate.

She does not appear in fashionable dress but in the soft drapery of a classical statue as if elevated to a realm beyond mundane reality. The artist has deliberately emphasised her goddess-like height by reducing the size of her head in proportion to her body and extending the line of her figure with a long flowing train.

The classical style of the masonry in the portrait mirrors the actual architecture of the orangery at Powis, which was built into the garden terraces in Mary's era. The orange trees that were cultivated in these glazed buildings were one of the great status symbols of the day.

Francis Grant (1803–78)
*Colonel, the Honourable
Percy Egerton Herbert
(1822–76)*
1857
Oil on canvas
140.3 x 110.5 cm

To thank

Most of the portraits at Powis show us how members of the Herbert family wished to be seen. This one tells us how they were seen by others.

The tablet at the bottom of this picture of Percy Egerton Herbert records that it was given to his mother Lucy, Countess of Powis by the tenants and neighbours of the Herberts' English estates. It was a gift in thanks for Percy's indefatigable service in the Crimean War in which he was wounded several times.

The bell tents stretching out into the distance represent the many soldiers whom he was responsible for provisioning as quartermaster-general of the British expeditionary forces in the Crimea.

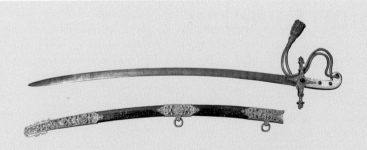

The ceremonial sword in the portrait was presented to Percy Egerton Herbert by Ludlow Corporation on 22 August 1856. It is decorated with diamonds, emeralds and rubies.

To bind together

Sometimes the material used to make a portrait sends a message in its own right.

Pastel likenesses were prized in the 18th century for their informality and tenderness, making them particularly suitable for intimate commissions destined for dressing rooms and bed chambers.

These sensitive pictures are the work of two artists working across two decades.

The adults depicted are Edward, Lord Clive (before he was made Earl of Powis), his wife Henrietta, and his brother and sister. They were drawn in Rome by the sought-after pastel specialist, Hamilton. The children are the sons and daughters of Edward and Henrietta, and were drawn several years later by their governess, Tonelli. She cleverly matched the backgrounds of her portraits to those of Hamilton's to create a single set that binds family members together across generations.

Above: Anna Tonelli (c.1763–1846)
Clockwise from top left: *The Honourable
Robert Henry Clive (1789–1854),
The Honourable Edward Clive (1785–1848),
Lady Henrietta Antonia Clive (1786–1835),
Lady Charlotte Florentia Clive (1787–1866)*
1794–7
Pastel on paper
24.5 x 19.7 cm

Opposite: Hugh Douglas Hamilton (1734–1806)
Clockwise from top left: *Edward Clive,
2nd Baron Clive of Plassey (1754–1839),
Lady Henrietta Clive, Baroness Clive of Plassey (1758–1830),
The Honourable Charlotte Clive (1762–95),
The Honourable Robert Clive (1769–1833)*
1788
Pastel on paper
24.5 x 19.7 cm

To promise

A portrait of a child fixes a transient stage of life in paint but can also carry with it a family's hopes for the future.

Gainsborough was a fashionable painter in the elegant resort of Bath when he painted this picture of Edward Clive. At the time it was commissioned, Edward's father, 'Clive of India', had recently been elevated from the gentry to the Irish peerage.

Suitably for the eldest son and heir of a newly noble family, Edward adopts the conventional pose of a courtier. The classical pillar and swag of brocade drapery are the traditional pictorial attributes of aristocracy in portraiture.

Touchingly, there is a hint of childhood vulnerability in this image of a budding nobleman. Wearing the ruffled collar and cropped hairstyle typical of a mid-18th-century schoolboy, Edward is dwarfed by his grand surroundings.

Thomas Gainsborough
(1727–1839)
The Honourable Edward Clive (1754–1839)
c.1762–3
Oil on canvas
127 x 101.6 cm

To valorise

In turbulent times, military prowess was one of the most important ways in which members of aristocratic families measured their achievements against those of their forebears.

Dating from the 1660s, Henry Herbert's portrait in armour with a red sash is reminiscent of that of his father, Richard, which was painted some three decades earlier. Henry's cool expression contrasts with the smoke and chaos of the battle unfolding in the background. This evokes his recent participation in the royalist rebellion of 1659, which presaged the restoration of the monarchy the following year.

Below: Gilbert Soest
(about 1605–81)
Henry Herbert (1640–91)
1660s
Oil on canvas
74.3 x 62.9 cm

Opposite: Cornelius
Johnson (1593–1661)
Richard Herbert
(c.1606–55)
1635
Oil on canvas
74.9 x 66.2 cm

To elevate

The ranks of the nobility were distinguished from one another at royal ceremonies by different styles of dress. The Herberts had themselves painted in their most formal portraits wearing these costumes to broadcast their rise up the hierarchy.

This portrait of Lady Elizabeth Herbert was painted when her husband, William, was created 1st Earl of Powis by Charles II. She dons a robe lined with ermine fur that only nobles and monarchs had a right to wear at court and has at her side a countess's distinctive coronet with pearls raised on golden stalks.

John Michael Wright
(1617–94)
*Lady Elizabeth Herbert,
Countess of Powis
(1633/4–91)*
c.1674
Oil on canvas
122.5 x 102.2 cm

In 1688, William and Elizabeth followed James II into exile in France where he continued to bestow honours on his loyal courtiers, although these were not recognised back in the British Isles. William, having been made a duke, is shown here in the ornate robes of the Order of the Garter. The picture was painted by the king's official painter around the time that William was inducted into this elite group, reserved for the monarch's closest allies.

François de Troy
(1645–1730)
William Herbert,
1st Marquess and
(titular) Duke of Powis
(1640–91)
c.1692
Oil on canvas
127 x 101.5 cm

British School
*Sir Edward Herbert, later
1st Baron Herbert of
Cherbury (1581/2–1648)*
17th century
Oil on canvas
73.5 x 61 cm

The many faces of Lord Herbert of Cherbury

Of all the members of the Herbert family represented in the pictures at Powis Castle, none used their image to promote their ends more intensively than the multifaceted Edward, 1st Baron Herbert of Cherbury.

Living in a courtly world in which great power was brokered through personal relationships, Lord Herbert understood that the highest rewards came to those talented few who could present themselves and their abilities with the greatest panache.

An unabashedly ambitious soldier, scholar, diplomat, musician and poet, he was a man of many parts and well aware of his worth. Portraits promoting the different aspects of his personality and achievements played an active role in his rise from son of a country gentleman to international statesman.

Foremost amongst these works of art is the miniature by the court artist, Isaac Oliver, whose attempt to capture the many layers of Lord Herbert's complex character in a single, exquisite likeness resulted in one of the masterpieces of British art (see page 38).

'If men get named for some one virtue; then,
What art thou, that art so many men ...'

Ben Jonson, Epigrams: 'To Sir Edward Herbert'

Timeline of the life of Lord Herbert of Cherbury

1581/2 Born to Richard and Magdalen Herbert of Montgomery Castle, Powys

1596 Begins studies at University of Oxford

1598 Marries older cousin Mary, heiress to Sir William Herbert of St Julians

1603 Made Knight of the Bath by James I at the accession and is painted in his crimson robes

1605 Becomes Sheriff and Member of Parliament for Montgomeryshire

1608 Visits the French royal court

1610 Joins Protestant forces in the Netherlands against the Spanish

Returns to London and is painted by William Larkin

1613–14 Painted by Isaac Oliver

1614 Re-joins Protestant forces in the Netherlands

1619 Becomes ambassador at the French court

1624 Recalled as ambassador to the French court

Created Baron of Castle Ireland in the Irish peerage

Publishes philosophical work *De Veritate* ('On truth')

1629 Created Lord Herbert of Cherbury

1631 Sculpted by Hubert Le Sueur

1632 Takes a seat on Charles I's Council of War

1642 Briefly imprisoned for loyalty to Charles I against Parliamentary forces

1643 Probably begins to write *Life of Herbert of Cherbury, Written by Himself*

1644 Surrenders Montgomery Castle to Parliamentary garrison

1648 Dies in London

1665 Poems posthumously published

Follower of William Larkin
(about 1585–1619)
*Sir Edward Herbert, later 1st
Baron Herbert of Cherbury
(1581/2–1648)*
c.1603
Oil on canvas
218.5 x 115 cm

Knight Errant

This is the earliest known portrait of Herbert and shows him as a handsome young gallant at court. He had been made a Knight of the Bath by James I in 1603, the year of the accession, and appears here in the official robes of that chivalric order.

In his autobiography he recalled that for the ceremony of investiture he had to *'weare Robes of Crimson Taffeta (in which habit I am painted in my study)'* referring to this portrait. With his usual bravado, he also noted that he could *'tell how much my person was commended by the Lords and Ladyes that came to see the Solemnitye'*.

The Latin motto in the top corner reads VIRTUS SIBI PRAETIUM meaning 'virtue is its own reward'. It is in the spirit of the oath Herbert made as a Knight *'never to sit in the place where injustice should bee done but they shall right it to the uttermost of their power and particularly Ladyes and Gentlewomen that shall be wronged in theire honour.'* It was a promise that he took seriously and was the cause of many a duel.

Divine hero

Herbert gave this picture to Sir Thomas Lucy (1585–1640) of Charlecote Park, Warwickshire where it remains to this day. It would have served as a memento of the events of 1609 when Herbert rescued Lucy from a sinking ship.

In his poetry, robes *'imbroidered with Starr-characters'* like the one draped over his shoulder signify providential destiny, so its presence here may be a reminder of the everlasting fame earned by such virtuous feats.

In 1610, Herbert was an emerging favourite at the royal courts of both France and England for just this kind of derring-do. Copies of this portrait, one of which is at Powis, helped establish Herbert as the man of the moment.

'Richard Earle of Dorset to whom otherwise I was a stranger, one day invited me to Dorset House … hee at last brought me to a Frame covered with greene Taffeta and asked mee who I thought was there and therewithall presently drawing the Courtaine shewed me my owne Picture whereupon demanding how his Lordship came have it, hee answered That he had heard soe many brave things of mee, That he had got a Coppy of a Picture which one Larkin a Painter drew for me.'

The Life of Lord Herbert of Cherbury, Written by Himself

Fearsome warrior

Herbert presents himself as a formidable man of war in this finely wrought bust by Le Sueur, King Charles I's court sculptor. The fierceness of his gaze is amplified by the masks of fantastical beasts that decorate his armour.

By the time this sculpture was made, Herbert was about 50 years old and had fought with distinction in several battles against the great Catholic powers. No longer the young darling of the court and somewhat disillusioned, Herbert's highest appointment as ambassador to France was now several years behind him.

But if Herbert hoped to catch the eye of Charles I by having a martial bust made by his official artist, the strategy worked. He was appointed a member of the King's Council of War the following year.

Hubert Le Sueur
(about 1580–1670)
Edward Herbert, 1st Baron Herbert of Cherbury (1581/2–1648)
1631
Bronze with wood socle
76 cm
Purchased with support of the Art Fund and National Heritage Memorial Fund

Opposite: William Larkin
(about 1585–1619)
Sir Edward Herbert, later 1st Baron Herbert of Cherbury (1581/2–1648)
c.1610
Oil on copper
55.9 x 45.7 cm
Charlecote Park, National Trust

The Oliver Miniature

Herbert was at the height of his glamour and held in *'greate Esteeme in Court and Citty'* when this miniature was painted in his early thirties. He had already distinguished himself in the violent field of war but was also sought after for his fast wit and learning borne of genuine scholarship.

The picture cleverly conveys several of these contrasting dimensions of his persona by depicting him poised between different worlds. High on a tranquil wooded hilltop, he is presented in a state of seclusion resting his head thoughtfully on his hand and stretching out alongside a stream.

Isaac Oliver
(about 1565–1617)
*Sir Edward Herbert, later
1st Baron Herbert of
Cherbury (1581/2–1648)*
c.1613–14
Watercolour on vellum
mounted on panel
18.1 x 22.9 cm

But the great world is waiting. In the background, his richly caparisoned horse paws impatiently at the ground while his squire prepares his armour so that he can take part in a jousting contest. Courtly display and power politics beckon and, beyond that, the lure of distant horizons and adventure.

Tiny details draw you closely in to this microcosm of a portrait, inviting you to marvel at the skill of its creation and the different facets of its remarkable subject.

Isaac Oliver
(about 1565–1617)
Self-Portrait
c.1590
Watercolour on vellum laid on card
4.5 x 3.7 cm
Royal Collection

Isaac Oliver was the official miniaturist of James I's queen, Anne of Denmark, when he painted Herbert. He distinguished himself by introducing new Continental European artistic ideas to the delicate traditions of the English miniature portrait. In his Herbert portrait, the Netherlandish-style landscape that stretches out into the far distance gives an innovative impression of depth.

Both pictures on this page are made of thin layers of watercolour on vellum (calf skin). Each individual element – face, costume, background – was completed separately. There was little room for error so the entire design must have been fully worked out in advance.

Melancholy heartthrob

All alone, lying down with his head propped
on his hand, Herbert adopts the classic pose of
a melancholy man. Understood as a disorder of
the mind and body, melancholy was diagnosed
by low spirits and tendency to moroseness.
It also enjoyed fashionable currency for its
other associations with creativity and the
pining of lovers.

His conspiratorial smile suggests that this
melancholy persona is as knowingly worn as
his artfully undone collar ribbons and dark curls.

Herbert was nothing if not aware of the seductive
charm of his image, which got him into trouble
more than once. At around this time he was stabbed
in the side by the jealous husband of one of Queen
Anne's ladies-in-waiting. She had been caught in
bed gazing at a miniature of Herbert that she had
commissioned from Oliver. Having set the picture
in gold and enamel she was in the habit of wearing
it *'about her neck soe lowe that she yet hid it under
her brestes'*.

Man-at-Arms

The squire in the background is preparing Herbert's armour. The brightness of the livery colours and the lance propped up on the tree reveal that Herbert is about to take part in a jousting tournament. These were one of the most splendid court entertainments of the day, expressing loyalty to the crown and harking back to medieval ideals of honour and valour.

These events also allowed courtiers to prove their martial skills. Important among these was mastery of the powerful cavalry horses that were used both in the jousting tilts and in the field of battle.

When in residence at his family house, Montgomery Castle, Herbert recalled that he *'passed some time, partly in studies and partly riding the great horse, of which I had a stable well-furnished: no horse yet was so dear to me as the Genet ['war horse'], I brought from France, whose love I had so Gotten that he would suffer none ere to ride him, more any many to come near him.'*

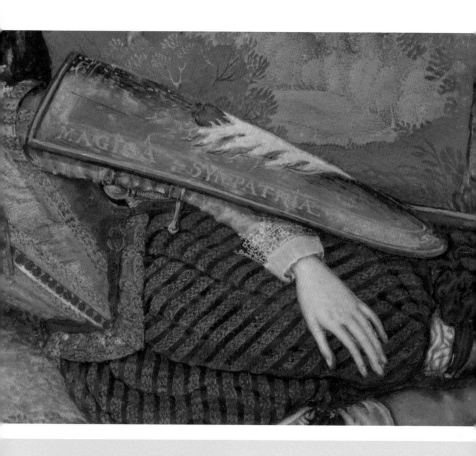

A stream and its source are depicted just below Herbert's arm. In the imagery of the time, springs stand for poetic inspiration. This may be an allusion to Herbert's skill in verse and his love of the lyric arts. His book of lute music, the only one of its kind compiled by a man, is held in the Fitzwilliam Museum, Cambridge.

Sage and poet

The shield on Herbert's arm is part of his jousting gear. These were always decorated with a combination of words (mottos) and images (devices) known as an impresas, and were designed by competing knights to express some personal quality or ideal. Herbert's motto is MAGICA SYMPATHIAE (Latin for 'sympathetic magic') and his device is a heart borne aloft by sparking flames. Both refer to his profound interest in philosophy.

According to the philosophy of Herbert's time, the universe was made up of countless correspondences between seemingly discrete entities. Sympathetic magic was the invisible force that connected all those objects together. Herbert would later publish works that developed this world view into theories about truth and the connectedness of the world's religions.

The image of the enflamed heart held different meanings. It could symbolise the immortality of the soul in heaven but also the burning desire of a lover for his mistress. In philosophy these could be reconciled through the ideal of Platonic love that saw worldly beauty as a fragment of the divine that could draw humans to virtue and godliness. Poets like Herbert, however, often subverted this idea, cleverly turning their verses on the subject of Platonic love into songs of seduction.

Impresas were often deliberately obscure so that knights' squires could reveal their meanings through verse recitations at tournaments. No such verses are known by Herbert to explain his impresa so it is unclear whether his evocation of magnetic forces and burning hearts is high-minded or seductive. The ambiguity, however, might be an intentional tease.

Find out more about portraits

Books

Marcia Pointon, *Portrayal and the Search for Identity*, Reaktion Books, 2012

Simon Schama, *The Face of Britain: The Nation through its Portraits*, Viking, 2015

Shearer West, *Portraiture*, Oxford University Press, 2004

Websites

National Portrait Gallery: www.npg.org.uk

Portrait of Britain (British Journal of Photography): www.portraitofbritain.uk

Tate: www.tate.org.uk/art/art-terms/p/portrait

Understanding British Portraits network: www.britishportraits.org.uk

Visit more portrait collections

National Trust Collections

Visit www.nationaltrustcollections.org.uk to delve deeper into the National Trust portrait and other collections.

Country houses

Attingham Park, Shropshire (National Trust)

Croft Castle, Herefordshire (National Trust)

Erddig, Wrexham (National Trust)

Weston Park, Shropshire

Museums

National Museum, Cardiff

The National Portrait Gallery, London

The Walker Art Gallery, Liverpool

Read more about Edward, Lord Herbert of Cherbury

Select writings

The Life of Edward, First Lord Herbert of Cherbury, Written by Himself, Oxford University Press, 1976

De Veritate, trans. Merick, H. Carré, J.W. Arrowsmith Ltd., 1937

The Poems: English and Latin, of Edward Lord Herbert of Cherbury, ed. G.C. Moore Smith, Clarendon Press, Oxford, 1923

Biographies

John A. Butler, *Lord Herbert of Chirbury: An Intellectual Biography,* Edwin Mellen Press, 1990

Ronald D. Bedford, *The Defence of Truth: Herbert of Cherbury and the Seventeenth Century,* Manchester University Press, 1979

About the author

Dr John Chu is Assistant Curator of Pictures and Sculpture for the National Trust. He has taught and published widely on British art and specialises in the art of Thomas Gainsborough and Joshua Reynolds.

Thank you for buying this guide. Your support helps us look after places like this.

Image credits